WEIRD-BUT-TRUE FACTS ABOUT WEATHER

The Child's World

Published by The Child's World®
1980 Lookout Drive • Mankato, MN 56003-1705
800-599-READ • www.childsworld.com

Acknowledgments
The Child's World®: Mary Berendes, Publishing Director
Red Line Editorial: Editorial direction
The Design Lab: Design
Amnet: Production

ISBN 9781614734239
LCCN 2012946530

Printed in the United States of America
Mankato, MN
November, 2012
PA02143

About the Author

Lauren Coss is a writer and editor living in Saint Paul, Minnesota. She loves learning new facts and watching a thunderstorm roll in—from a safe place, of course!

About the Illustrator

A former greeting card artist, Mernie Gallagher-Cole is a freelance illustrator with over 28 years experience illustrating for children. Her charming illustrations can be found on greeting cards, party goods, games, puzzles, children's books, and now e-books and educational game apps! She lives in Philadelphia with her husband and two children.

TABLE OF CONTENTS

INTRODUCTION

Earth's weather has sudden swings and crazy highs and lows. It can be wet, windy, cold, or hot. It can change on a moment's notice. From the icy polar regions to the steamy tropics, weather on Earth is never dull! Get ready for a flood of some of the most fascinating weather facts around. They may seem strange or unbelievable, but remember, they are all true!

Bess

Edna

RAIN AND HAIL AND SNOW, OH MY!

There are places on Earth that have never seen rain.

The Atacama Desert in Chile is the driest place on Earth. Some parts of the desert have not had a single drop of rain since people began keeping records.

It has never rained cats and dogs, but it has rained frogs and fish.

Scientists believe this unusual weather occurs when strong winds caused by hurricanes and water tornadoes pick up the creatures. Then the storm drops them on unsuspecting cities nearby.

Rain can fall out of a clear blue sky.

Raindrops can be carried for many miles, so rain can fall even if no clouds can be seen. Keep that umbrella handy!

Rain comes in red and yellow colors.

The yellow is most likely caused by pollen particles suspended in the water drops. Red rain is most likely caused by reddish dust. **Algae** in the rainwater might have caused red rain in India in 2001. These unusual rains look faintly colored, but they do not stain anything.

The largest hailstone ever found in the United States was as big as a soccer ball.

The huge chunk of ice landed in Aurora, Nebraska, in 2003. It measured more than 18 inches (45 cm) around. Luckily, it didn't hit anyone as it crashed to the ground!

It hails an average of 132 days a year in Kericho, Kenya.

That means this city, located not too far from the equator, gets hail more than one-third of the year!

In 1959, a hailstorm in Seldon, Kansas, covered the city with 1.5 feet (.5 m) of ice.

The storm lasted 85 minutes and stopped cars on the highway for four hours.

A baseball-sized piece of hail falls as fast as a professional baseball pitcher can throw.

A piece of ice this size can fall at speeds of 100 miles per hour (160 km/h).

Mountain snow can turn the color of a watermelon.

This pink snow is caused by a kind of algae. It is most common at a high **altitude**, such as in the mountains of California. Some hikers have even claimed the snow smells sweet like watermelon juice.

It has snowed in every U.S. state, even Florida !

The sunshine state got more than one-half foot (.2 m) of snow during a blizzard that struck the East Coast in 1993.

More than two-thirds of people in the world have never seen snow.

The largest snowflake was the size of a hubcap.

The giant flake was reported at 15 inches (38 cm) wide and 8 inches (20 cm) thick. It fell in Montana in 1887. However, no scientist was able to verify it. The largest verified snowflake was 8 by 12 inches (20 by 30 cm). It fell in Siberia in 1971.

The world's tallest snowman was actually a snowwoman.

Olympia the snowwoman was built in Bethel, Maine, in 2008. At 12 stories tall, she towered over the town. Her eyelashes were made of snow skis.

Snowflakes fall about as fast as you walk.

From about 2 miles (3 km) high in the sky, it takes a snowflake approximately an hour to reach the ground.

Silver Lake, Colorado, got enough snow in one day to bury cars.

In mid-April 1921, the mountain town got 75.8 inches (192.5 cm) of snow in just 24 hours. That's more than 6 feet (1.8 m)!

Antarctica is actually a huge desert.

The icy southern continent receives an average of less than 2 inches (5.1 cm) of **precipitation** a year.

LIGHTNING STRIKES AGAIN

The odds are 1 in 3,000 that you will be struck by lightning— unless your name is Roy Sullivan.

This unlucky park ranger was struck by lightning a world-record seven times. Lightning knocked off one of his toenails. Another time, it set his hair on fire.

Most lightning strikes on land, not water.

Nine out of ten lightning bolts strike land, even though Earth's surface area is more than 70 percent water.

The longest measured lightning bolt was 118 miles (190 km) long.

An average lightning bolt is 3 to 5 miles (4.8 to 8 km) long.

Every second, the Earth is being zapped by about 100 lightning bolts.

Tall buildings such as the Empire State Building can be struck by lightning more than 15 times during a single storm.

Lightning sometimes bakes potatoes.

When lightning strikes farmers' fields, it can heat up and damage the plants there, including potatoes.

The average bolt of lightning has enough energy to power a 100-watt light bulb for more than three months.

Lightning can strike when the sun is shining.

One lightning bolt can travel more than 60 miles (96 km). That means it can strike far away from the center of a thunderstorm.

WILD, WET, AND WINDY

If you see cows start to lie down, a storm might be coming.

Pressure in the atmosphere decreases before a storm. This pressure change can affect a cow's digestive system. This makes the cow uncomfortable, often making it lie down.

If you think bad weather makes the day seem longer, you might be right.

According to scientists, changes in wind speed can actually slow down the Earth's rotation very slightly. Earthquakes can have the same effect. The change is just a fraction of a second. But it is enough that scientists add a leap second once every several years to make up the difference.

There has always been the same amount of water on Earth.

The water cycle is a closed system. That means you might be drinking the same water as Cleopatra or even the dinosaurs.

One weather phenomenon looks like a rainbow that has been set on fire.

This phenomenon is actually an ice-halo. It happens when the sun hits ice crystals in the sky in the right way.

In the desert, wild winds can whip up dust storms more than one-half mile (1 km) high.

These sandstorms are called haboobs. They often happen with a thunderstorm.

Wildfires can actually cause tornadoes.

These fire tornadoes occur when the rising heat from a fire mixes with rotating air. The tornadoes spread ashes and embers, causing the fire to spread.

Black blizzards darkened the skies in the United States in the 1930s.

An intense drought struck the Midwestern plains in an area that would be called the Dust Bowl. Overplowing had caused extreme **erosion**, sending dust and dirt into the sky. Winds whipped the dust across the land, destroying crops. In some places the dust even buried houses.

The fastest wind ever recorded was 231 miles per hour (372 km/h).

The mighty gust swept across Mount Washington in New Hampshire on April 12, 1934.

Tornadoes have been seen on every continent except Antarctica.

The Southeast Asian country of Bangladesh has the most tornadoes in the world outside of North America. The United States and Canada top the list.

A single tornado touched three states in 1925.

Known as the tristate tornado, the storm traveled for 219 miles (352 km). It began in Missouri and traveled across Illinois and into Indiana.

Of all the tornadoes in the world, three-quarters of them occur in the United States.

The most likely place to get hit by a tornado is 2 miles (3 km) east of Giltner, Nebraska.

Tornadoes are the ultimate pickle transporter.

In 1917, a Connecticut tornado picked up a jar of pickles. The pickles were found in a ditch 25 miles (40 km) away. The jar was unbroken!

Hurricanes started getting names during World War II.

U.S. Navy and Air Force meteorologists named the storms after their wives and girlfriends. Today, the names go in alphabetical order and alternate between male and female names.

A hurricane releases the energy of a ten-megaton nuclear bomb every 20 minutes.

Hurricanes in the Northern Hemisphere always rotate counterclockwise.

In the Southern Hemisphere they rotate clockwise.

Earth is not the only planet with hurricanes.

Jupiter's hurricanes make Earth's weather look tame. One Jupiter hurricane has been raging for more than 300 years. It is bigger than Earth!

HOT AND COLD

The warmest temperature ever recorded in Antarctica was a balmy 59 degrees Fahrenheit (15°C).

The winter of 1899 was so cold that the Mississippi River froze solid from Minnesota to Illinois.

Ice chunks were reported as far south as the Gulf of Mexico.

The most recent ice age is happening right now.

According to scientists, an ice age is defined as any time the Earth has polar ice caps, and right now it does.

In 1995, it was so hot in Missouri that bales of hay burst into flames.

The freshly cut hay released a gas called methane. The gas eventually got so hot it burst into flames, burning the hay with it.

The coldest temperature recorded in the solar system was in Finland.

But it did not happen naturally. In 2000, scientists cooled a metal called rhodium to a chilling –459 degrees Fahrenheit (–237°C). The second coldest temperature ever recorded in the solar system was –455 degrees Fahrenheit (–235°C), on Neptune's moon Triton.

The coldest natural temperature on Earth was – 129 degrees Fahrenheit (– 89°C).

The temperature was recorded in 1983 at the Volstok Station in Antarctica.

Only two U.S. states have never recorded a temperature above 100 degrees Fahrenheit (38°C): Alaska and Hawaii.

The hottest place in the United States is Death Valley, California, with a high temperature of 134 degrees Fahrenheit (56.7°C) in 1913.

The hottest natural temperature ever recorded was 136 degrees Fahrenheit (57°C).

The temperature was recorded at Al Azizia, Libya, in 1922.

GLOSSARY

algae (AL-jee)
Algae are small plants that do not have any roots or stems and usually grow in water. Sometimes, algae can make rainwater look red or snow look pink.

altitude (AL-ti-tood)
Altitude measures height from the ground or sea level. Pink snow usually occurs at a very high altitude.

erosion (i-ROH-zhuhn)
Erosion is the wearing away of something due to water, wind, or other causes. Too much erosion can cause dust storms.

hemisphere (HEM-i-sfeer)
One half of a round object is a hemisphere. Earth has a Northern Hemisphere and a Southern Hemisphere.

phenomenon (fuh-NAH-muh-nahn)
A phenomenon is a fact or event that can be seen or experienced. An ice-halo is an amazing phenomenon to witness.

precipitation (pri-sip-i-TAY-shuhn)
Precipitation is any form of water that falls from the sky, including rain, sleet, hail, or snow. Antarctica gets very little precipitation.

LEARN MORE

BOOKS

Furgang, Kathy. *National Geographic Kids Everything Weather: Facts, Photos, and Fun that Will Blow You Away.* Washington, DC: National Geographic, 2012.

Prokos, Anna. *Tornadoes.* Pleasantville, NY: Gareth Stevens, 2009.

Rotter, Charles. *Hurricanes: Storms of the Sea.* Mankato, MN: Creative Education, 2003.

WEB SITES

Visit our Web site for links about weird weather facts: **childsworld.com/links**

Note to Parents, Teachers, and Librarians: We routinely verify our Web links to make sure they are safe and active sites. So encourage your readers to check them out!

INDEX